PENDULUM

The Poetry of Dreams

An Anthology of Modern Verse

AVALANCHE BOOKS

Published in Great Britain by Avalanche Books, England. 2008.

Printed by SRP, England

The moral rights of the authors have been asserted.

British Library Cataloguing in Publication Data. A catalogue record for this book is available from the British Library.

ISBN 978 1 874392 42 2

ACKNOWLEDGEMENTS

"Reporting For Duty", "Remembrance", "I Departed
the Fetid House of My Fathers When Even the Fawning
Stench Could not Persuade Them to Change Their Name",
"The Long Day Has Fallen", "Vista", "In Praise of Despair",
"Harbour Days" and "The Count" from "Seasons of Winter"
by Chris Tutton, published by Avalanche Books. "Daffodils"
and "The Unanswered Call" from "Rain Angel" by Chris
Tutton, published by Avalanche Books. "The Catcher's Tap",
"Fama's Bequest" and "Stygian Shore" from "Ecumenical
Shadows" by Chris Tutton, published by Avalanche Books.
"Mystical Mother", "If", "Cutting the Population" and
"The Fridge Frees Yer" from "Full Metal Jacket Potato"
by Marvin Cheeseman, published by The Bad Press.
"Nancy's Dream" and "The Disappearing" from "The
Dog in the Sky" by Helen Ivory, published by Bloodaxe
Books (February 2006)
"A Dream of Honey" from "Sanctuary" by Matthew
Sweeney, published by Jonathan Cape. Reprinted by
permission of The Random House Group.
"Dunstanburgh" (*excerpt*) by Katrina Porteous first
published by Smokestack Books and commissioned by
BBC Radio

"Remembrance" by Chris Tutton has appeared in "Morden
Poets". "Creation" by Helen Ivory has appeared in
"Seam" "On a February Night" by Alison Brackenbury has
appeared in "Poetry Review". "Fans" by Matthew Sweeney has
appeared in "Manuscripte" (Austria) "Post-Market" and "The
High-Rise Flats" by Kostas Hrisos have appeared in "Morden
Poets". "Cut" by Martin Figura has appeared in "Seam".
"Trip to the Admission Ward", "The Bath" and "The Weight" by
Martin Figura have appeared in "The Same" (USA)

FOREWORD
by Deborah Gaye

Dreams have always played an important role in poetry, story-
telling and oral tradition; from Homer, through to the medieval
dream poetry of Chaucer and Langland, and to poets of the
modern day.

The multi faceted, multi-layered landscapes of dreams and
dreaming are central to Pendulum, which is sub-titled 'The
Poetry of Dreams'. In it I have sought to represent the cream of
contemporary British poetry, by bringing together some of its
leading lights to create an atmosphere of the magical.

The often devastating and yearning quality of dreams is beauty-
fully and hauntingly expressed in the dark, richly romantic and
metaphysical imagery of Chris Tutton; the transcendental lyricism
of Pascale Petit, Helen Ivory, Philip Gross and Fiona Sampson,
and the 'alternative realism' (a term he proposed himself) of
Matthew Sweeney.

In order to retain a sense of balance and spontaneity, and to
prevent the collection from becoming as nocturnal as it may have
otherwise, it must be said that not every piece here is conspicuously
connected to the dreams of sleep. However, many of those which
are not are imbued with the atmosphere of reverie, as in the
deliciously wistful musings of Roselle Angwin, and the eloquent
commentary on modern values and attitudes unequivocal
in the observations of Nii Ayikwei Parkes, Kostas Hrisos, Martin
Figura and Maya Chowdhry, speak of dreams for a collective
conscience. The timeless and universal themes of love and loss,
of hope and despair, are meticulously captured in the exquisite
verses of Alison Brackenbury, Paul Sutherland and Joolz Denby,
while Katrina Porteous writes with aching serenity of the natural
landscape and our place within it. Roz Goddard and John Siddique
soulfully reflect on fears and relationships, and Philip Coker and

David Hendtlass write of dreams and absence with subtle wit and sublime tenderness. The collection is perfectly rounded and lightened by the insouciant, quirky humour of Marvin Cheeseman.

Unlike many other anthologies, themed or otherwise, I believe the consistent quality and genuinely complimentary styles of the featured poets combine to provide a wonderful, dreamlike fluidity and readability. I would like to extend my heart felt gratitude to all the writers here who, to a person, gave their mainly unpublished work and support so generously and enthusiastically. They have combined to produce a body of work which is as powerful as the most vivid dream. They truly are dream poets. I believe they represent the very best of their genre.

Critics of Walter de la Mare admired him for expressing "a hint of the magical in the midst of modernity" and it is, perhaps, this sentiment above all others that I have hoped to bring to this anthology.

Contents

TO MARGINS

and nameless places

to that twig quivering
where the bird
isn't

to the tilt of our lives
towards
and away from
each other

to words
and to
speaking without them

Roselle Angwin

REPORTING FOR DUTY

The small boy's father dreamed of the sea like
A lover dreams of the scent of skin.
It didn't matter which sea. Any would do:
He needed to escape.
The small boy never dreamed of the sea.
Mostly he dreamed of his father and of
Being a father like him.
One day the small boy watched his father
Wake from a customary short
Summer Sunday afternoon siesta
And soon after quietly asked:
'What did you dream, father?'
His father looked kindly at the small boy and
Answered unhesitatingly:
'I always dream of you, my son', he purred,
Folding corners of the morning newspaper
Into a sailboat.

Chris Tutton

THE UNANSWERED CALL

Silently, inexorably,
Black dogs lost on the
Dark side of night
We lose scent of the chase
In torched fields where we
Leave each other wandering.

Chris Tutton

DAFFODILS
for Ray

Hawthorn fringed this
                        Scrub
A nursery once
We coursed contours of spiked
                        Green
Circumventing flowerbeds
In scuffed shoes

Golden brocade spanned this
                        Hill
A spring of daffodils seeped
And we ran until blooms
                        Became
Empty spaces
Framed by footprints.

Chris Tutton

15

REMEMBRANCE

There are shapes in this sand no tide will fill
Nor any breeze blow nameless into night
And wandering sleepless moments when you
Amble homeward beside me casting no
Glance nor word nor shadow beneath
Broken cinnamon moonshine
Spilling like a thistle in the
Blister of the distance between us.

Chris Tutton

STYGIAN SHORE

I watch you from the beach of dreams
Moonlit on feldspar crags where
Quiet breezes keep your bronze tresses
Lapping your neck like a midnight tide.

Chris Tutton

TREE OF THE WORLD

On nights when the sounds of the children
we should have had wake me, I sit in the yellow
of the bulb, and place my hands upon the horizon,
spin on the axis mundi which connects us,

even though at times we have no desire to be connected.
The stones on the moor, touched by so many
over the centuries, will speak our confessions,
if we will just stand, lay our hands and listen at the centre.

The carvings of spirals and swastikas, concentric rings
and bloodlines, added to over millennia, will fade
in eternity's face. Each year a wipe of a cloth over rough stone.
Soon they'll be polished and faceless, then sand on the wind.

I will wait for you there, where the symbols
lose their meanings, where our attempts
at holding on are less than nothings, but still the axis,
nameless and unspeakable, is true, never out of sight.

John Siddique

DAVID

It's fourteen years since that New York spring,
when we arrived in full snow. Travelled north
to retreat, made sheet ice sculptures on the lake
with the view of the atomic power station.

Just as the thaw melts the white world, we're driving,
invited to stay in the city of towers.
A small sliver of a flat in Greenwich Village,
all night coffee crowds, real live porn on tv.

From up the Empire State you can see everything.
From the World Trade Centre you can see even more.
Below us the building is half empty, scrappy offices,
rooms too numerous to fill.

We were eagles casting shadows with our hands
on the harbour, dream-catchers on this observation platform.
Bridges span the brown river. We were great friends then,
trying to photograph 360 degrees, friends with shared beliefs.

Trying to start ahead of ourselves. Making statements
and precepts to right the world instead of being ourselves.
There was no parting, or angry words. Our foundations
were built on speeches. Some friendships are like family,
ours was a series of agreements.
We agreed for a decade, then one day we didn't.

John Siddique

SUMMER CYCLE # 2

I wake in the television static of 3.40.
A voice on the phone, then it's gone,
she'd misdialed an old number.

I'd forgotten the sound of her voice.
I think about my family back home
and I let her sound play through me.
She's in a new world; new friends, a new husband.
I'm a new beginning, though something keeps me
moving from place to place with work.

In vague and familiar rooms, we'll
take up new lives, while the spider's web
of inferences spun in the night hangs
jewelled with moisture under the windowsill,
connecting wood and stone with its threads.
Almost translucent. Strong and ready.

John Siddique

SALMON

The moon was coming up one side of the river
and the sun was setting on the other
when a huge salmon leapt

from the shock of whitewater. On his left flank
his scales shimmered with moonlight,
on his right they blazed with sun.

He seemed to hang there in the air
in pyjamas of pearl and ash,
half a wedding-suit of rosefire.

I thought of you asleep in the cabin
and rushed home to look
as sunset's last rays costumed your back

through one window, and the full moon
robed your chest through the other. You jumped
as if you'd leapt out of yourself

and were heading upstream. For a moment
you hung there, half out of your skin,
your body lost in the shadows.

Pascale Petit

BABY MOON

We've hung a baby moon in a birdcage
from our bedroom ceiling.

We climb a silver birch ladder
to feed her star gruel.

She cries a lot, wants the window left open
so a breeze will rock her.

Each month she grows thin and vanishes.
When she's full, her light floods our bed.

We lie under her like two squid,
our skins flickering with seas.

Pascale Petit

SELF-PORTRAIT WITH CROPPED HAIR
after Frida Kahlo

I listened to the grinding of obsidian blades
in that sixth room of hell
I fell into after you left.
I sharpened the scissors until
my bedroom became the House of Knives.

Then I sat on the crazy-yellow chair
and painted my black snake-locks rising
from the floor. I watched them dance like musical staves
and sing that old folksong you used to whistle –

Look, if I love you, it is for your hair,
now you are bald I love you no more.

Pascale Petit

THE DREAM
after Frida Kahlo

Embalmed, my face is a mask grey with rain.

I have not disappeared.
My toes have fallen off.

I am a parrot with nothing left to say.

I, the atrocity,
more naked than a human should be,

a sideshow girl with gold islands in her flesh –
sawdust, greasepaint, sequins,

my canopied bed left on the gallery floor.

Out the ambulance window – a stalled harbour,
water the texture of confusion.

I am the river coming home,
waves rising and falling like clear glass bells.

Pascale Petit

23

ATTITUDES OF PRAYER

Nothing raised.
Rather, a stooped gathering –
think of the stoop of back
                     over a sink

and gathered, baled-up lengths of cotton, drawn up
          against the weight of water,
the counter-sprawl
          of its own white wings –

Water thickening the fabric to transparency
          makes a liquid lens between the threads;
                              a widening glue
as if the sheet might blur, dissolve.

Yet all the time
its almost-bodily weight tugging on dorsal muscles.
          Like a Pieta.

It's what they lack, those luminous masters
who understood
                     the way of beauty is the way
of the Cross

but missed
          its sheer weight:
how body thickens self
into the world –

Light from the kitchen window
falls like news across white knuckles, white fabric
now bundled, now spread
in the steel sink.
                    This pipe-thrum
is an echo of holiness.

*

Adolescent, she stoops
as if lifting the ground
like a cover
            up to her chin.

Down the tree-lined street
darkness gathers in quiffs of grass,
under parked cars;
            the smell of damp
at a window –

*

The stoop of attention. Craning –
                              downward
or sideways –
the spine, that white plumb-line,
                              strains,
making space or measuring space.
            Inwards.

Now the stoop's an opening,

exposes
>layers of possibility:

think about the heart-shaped back,
both surface and turn –
>the flare or close of a shoulder,
>lower vertebrae
>>buttoning skin –
how it folds over,
>but never shuts.

The line's proffered, and held:
Interior with Nude; Woman Bathing.

*

A bent back
>sends space upward
like prayer, to a whitewashed ceiling.
The sky beyond wheeling with swifts.

In an upstairs room, a mattress is lifted, covered;
fills the arms like a body.
A sheet billows and flares
>and falls short;

now kneeling, now rising
to bend across her work,
a woman unfolds cotton and smoothes it.

The clean sheet
opens a white pane in the house.

All day it lies in an empty room,
smelling of sunlight
                and aloe vera.
As light fades, it collects pallor:
intensifying, deepening.

        When she no longer seems possible
the woman returns.
A movement among shadows,
she comes to the bed,
                stoops tenderly –

she must haul up some form of meaning
                thread after thread.

Fiona Sampson

ST KILDA'S WREN

I thought you said rain. You said wren,
Small haunter of bog and lichen,
Loud as gulls' laughter, fierce as men.

Let me guess. Who was St Kilda?
A stout woman, like my milder
Aunts? A man? The rain blows wilder.

The Middle Ages made names up,
Saints, authorities, a cup
Flashed gold from iron, at will. Just step

On to the railway bank. The bird
Flits down, swollen, small brown word.
The male, who wove each nest, is heard

Shrilled, triumphant, darts up when
Other birds shrink from storm or fen,
Shouts to the saintless. Rain, wren, wren.

Alison Brackenbury

LAPWINGS

They were everywhere. No. Just God or smoke
Is that. They were the backdrop to the road,

My parents' home, the heavy winter fields
From which they flashed and kindled and uprode

The air in dozens. I ignored them all.
"What are they?" "Oh – peewits –" Then a hare flowed,

Bounded the furrows. Marriage. Child. I roamed
Round other farms. I only knew them gone

When, out of a sad winter, one returned.
I heard the high mocked cry "Pee – <u>wit</u>," so long

Cut dead. I watched it buckle from vast air
To lure hawks from its chicks. That time had gone.

Gravely, the parents bobbed their strip of stubble.
How had I let this green and purple pass?

Fringed, plumed heads (full name, the crested plover)
Fluttered. So crowned cranes stalk Kenyan grass.

Then their one child, their anxious care, came running
Squeaked along each furrow, daft and dauntless.

Did I once know the story of their lives?
Do they migrate from Spain? Or coasts' cold run?

And I forgot their massive arcs of wing.
When their raw cries swept over, my head spun

With all the brilliance of their black and white
As though you cracked the dark and found the sun.

Alison Brackenbury

AT 53

I claim to have forgotten nothing,
birthdays, my list, the piece of cake
in the corner cupboard
delicately dry.

Here is my list: but note above
that I have lost my first cat's name,
shed keys,
three gloves
and how to love.

Alison Brackenbury

I'VE JUST HAD THE STRANGEST DREAM

I once had a dream about Clement Freud
Hard to believe but it's true
On the night of the second of April
In the year two-thousand and two.

It's hard to remember much detail
Though he'd asked me to make him some tea
He wanted Earl Grey or Darjeeling
But all I had in was P.G.

His bald head was shining quite brightly
(Clement wasn't wearing a hat)
I once had a dream about Clement Freud
You can't get more Freudian than that.

Marvin Cheeseman

IF

If you can lose you hair when all about you
Are keeping theirs and laughing loud at you
Yet not let wigs or transplants ever tempt you
And not let baldness leave you feeling blue
If you can take real pride in your appearance
If you can work and not be scared to graft
If you can show relentless perseverance
Whilst colleagues arse about and just act daft

If you can put up shelves that last for ages
And help your neighbours decorate for days
Knowing that you won't get any wages
Or even hear one single word of praise
If you can spend your weekends in IKEA
If you can do the things that please your wife
Then shamelessly pretend you've no idea
How your mate lets football dominate his life

If you can make one heap of all your earnings
And risk it on one horse picked with a pin
And never brag despite the constant yearnings
Or breathe a word of your colossal win
If you can turn your back on television
Not just to spend your free time getting pissed
And later not regret your brave decision
When you hear of all the cracking things you've missed

If you can sail a ship across the ocean
Or fly a jet and through the heavens climb
Become an astronaut through pure devotion
Or at least just pass your driving test first time
If you can do these things I've never mastered
And still get home in time to make the tea
Perhaps you'll be a smug obnoxious bastard
But son you'll be a better man than me.

Marvin Cheeseman

ON THE SUPERIOR NATURE OF FOSSIL FUELS

There's no fuel…

…. like an old fuel.

Marvin Cheeseman

THREE ANOMALIES

1.

The only still man in Spitalfields market,
maybe in all London, with a rust of stubble,
            rag of oilcloth for a poncho,
and good shoes… not begging, he holds nothing
but his ground, his focus on some distance. John

the Baptist? King Cnut with the waves? A rock
in the swash and backwash of us, he's the snag
            that slits the fabric of the crowd
so it can't heal; he's the lump of a question
that sticks in a busy day's throat. If he would only

speak. But he's *using* us – a penance, or to school
himself to be untouched, to rise stone-dry
            from the flood. What we make
of him won't matter, when he masters it. Too
late already to ask. Don't look back. Swirl on by.

2.

One stands up naked
in a crowded room
with a small Buddha smile.
This is one of those dreams,

he says. *I am a lucid dreamer.*
Speaking thus, he leaves.

No help for the rest of us, then.
(The sideways glance. *I could
have sworn...* The urge to run home
and phone a friend at random:

Where was I just now? Prove it.)
So no one says a word,

which confirms every doubt.
(On the other hand, where
is *he* now? Is he watching
the hour hand track round,

his certainty slipping: *God,
what if I* don't *wake up soon?)*

3.

She turns round on the rush-hour escalator,
  right in front of you.

It's as if she'd forgotten something,
  as if everybody had –

like a premonition, the first whiff, too fine
  for the conscious mind,

of scorching. But isn't this just what
  you wished for, once:

the Zen man's *Ah?* Yes but, please,
  not so sudden, not like this,

eye to eye with that look like the crack
  of the one pair of wings

on the salt marsh, that raises the flock
  collapsing upwards to the sky

like a card house in reverse. Not
  here, not now. But now

is all you have to grasp her word-
  less question, and reply.

Philip Gross

PAST BEDTIME

A February Spring, out of all
right order
          and a night that glows

with clumps of primroses startled
awake by streetlight… Here's me,

and a cat, and a cat (they have
no plural).
          In bungalow streets

the going down of dimmer switches,
pinching-out of lights behind the louvred blinds…

I'm still thinking of one window, wide-
eyed-innocent, that I passed a while back

open on a plumped-up bed: pale blues,
pinks, pompoms and a panoply of soft-

stuffed floppities: bears, pups, bunnies
but most of all seals, more baby-black-eyes

angled skywards than seemed right.
Too arranged, too untouched.
                    For the grandchildren,

I tell myself, still on their journey – a beacon
left lit to bring in or bring back the small ones

like moths from the night
                              but it's late,
late and I don't think they're coming

and it's past their bedtimes anyway.

Philip Gross

FANS

Seven horses climbed out of the Wannsee
and galloped, dripping, to Kleist's grave.
They neighed and bent their forelegs –
one rapped the stone gently with a hoof,
another came forward to lick the name.
Then, one by one, they felt a weight
drop on their backs, and a jab in the side
poke them into a joyful canter along
the big lake's bank. Such whinnying
had not been heard for centuries, thought
a man walking three barking terriers.
When each horse returned another left
till all seven had felt the rider's weight
then they stood in a ring around the grave
to neigh a soft, high-pitched chorus
before pulling off in strict formation
to trot in a row, heads high, back to where
they'd left the water, wade in again,
watched by a group of shrieking kids, then
swim in an arc towards the farther shore.

Matthew Sweeney

A DREAM OF HONEY

I dreamed that bees were extinct,
had been for decades, and honey
was a fabled memory, except for jars
hoarded by ancient, wealthy gourmets.
Honey was still on the shelves, of course –
that's what they'd named the sweet concoction
chemists had arrived at, and it sold well,
not just to those who knew no better,
and the day was coming fast when no one
alive would be able to taste the difference.

Then one Friday morning in Riga
a peasant woman arrived by horse and cart
at the old Zeppelin Hangars market
and set up her stall with jars of honey
flavoured by the various flowers. Around her
sellers of the new honey gawped, then sniffed
as she screwed the lids off, then glared
as her jars were snapped up in minutes,
and she climbed on her cart again
and let the horse take her away.

In the dream, e-mails sped everywhere
about this resurrection of honey,
and supermarket-suppliers scoured Latvia,
knocking on every door, sending helicopters
low over houses, looking for beehives,
but after a month they gave it up,
and the woman never appeared again

though rumours of her honey-selling
came over the border from Russia
and continued beyond the dream.

Matthew Sweeney

FRAGILE

The blue vase cracked and fell apart.
I lifted the shards from the glass table,
then a Henry Miller painting left the wall,
its glass front smashing on impact.
In the mirror I saw the Picasso urn wobbling.
I dived for it, like a goalkeeper, or bodyguard,
grabbed it, and the other Picasso pieces,
to bury among the cushions of the settee.
I looked around at the marble table lamps,
the ornate clock on the mantelpiece,
the black dogs on the Chinese secretaire,
the framed photographs on the wall –
all had to be laid out on the carpet.
Then I went and dropped the eau-de-vie.

Matthew Sweeney

NANCY'S DREAM

Her dead husband is learning to fly.
Daylight flights are fine
but it's wartime, so night flights
are impossible with the black-outs.

She's fretting about how he will ever land
and when the sirens go off
she worries about how they know
these are enemy planes over head.

He could be up there, in the middle
of all the stars and the moon-washed clouds
with the homing pigeons whose
houses have been destroyed by the bombing.

He could be up there with a lock of her hair
in that envelope scented with lavender
flying aimlessly in the dark,
and not being able to land, not ever.

Helen Ivory

CREATION

On the third day, she draws the sun
into her mouth and swallows it whole.
It glows in her throat, sinks down
to her stomach, bubbles through
her insides, like molten gold.

On the fourth day, she lets the moon
enter her, plant its seed in her womb,
grows its silver children, till strong enough
to swim into the nightlong sky,
and take their place among the heavens.

On the fifth day she takes the sea into her hands,
runs it through her fingers like silk.
She puts fishes into coral baskets for her children;
waits for them to haul them up
to fill their greedy mouths.

On the sixth day, she cuts her skin
with her own sharpened nails, drips blood
into deep black earth, falls to her knees.
She watches trees and animals grow up
from the ground as she becomes weaker.

On the seventh day, she is barely breathing.
She hears the postman and the phone
that keeps ringing. She is aware of a light,
which she thinks is the sun, burning her eyes.
For two days, for two days, she rests.

Helen Ivory

DREAMING

Then awake to a disjointed sky
and not enough light.

Your breathing is so hushed
and you are cast out miles.

I pick my way
through the messy bedroom floor,

unearth your phone;
resist the urge to check your calls.

Helen Ivory

THE DISAPPEARING

Slowly he watched her disappear:
The empty pile where there used to be ironing,
the absence of lipstick on her coffee cup,
the plants, dry from wanting.

Her conversation became vague:
she would sit motionless in front of unlit fires,
talking in circles about boats she once owned
and lions that ate from the palm of her hand.

At the start of her disappearing,
she would spend all day in the kitchen,
whisking up exotic meals from recipes
she said she'd learned from foreign shores.

But as her disappearing became more pronounced,
she avoided the kitchen entirely.
So he made sturdy broths to feed her up
when her bones began to show.

Although by now she had stopped talking,
she would stand at the tall window,
dreamily singing songs he'd never heard;
songs that sounded less and less like earthly music.

One morning, when he was on the edge of sleep,
a soft fluttering sound persuaded him awake.
And there she was – a translucent shape
hovering at the open window.

He tried hopelessly to catch her ankle
as she drifted outside into the dawn light,
where already birds in their thousands
were gathering in the sky.

Helen Ivory

SLEEP

In this house, everything sleeps.
Even the walls have relaxed
and the roof is too tired
to hold up the weight of the sky.

It is so long since the front door
has opened, the skin has grown over.
The postman has given up
looking for the letter-box.

The girl in the room upstairs
is a woman now. In waking moments,
she sleep-walks to the mirror,
takes a brush to the long silk of her hair.

Before she lies down again, she'll notice
the bird skulls on the window sill,
how cobwebs have laced them together,
how her face has grown sharp as a knife.

Helen Ivory

THE CATCHER'S TAP

The old man slept shaded on the bank of the river and dreamed of a time when he was young. In the afternoon he always slept because the sun was too hot and the reflected light upon the water hurt his eyes. On the path, not far from the old man, walked a small boy with a butterfly cupped in the palm of his hand. As he glanced down from behind a thicket of golden curls, the small boy noticed that the old man had left the door to his soul ajar. Almost at once the small boy released the butterfly, tapped lightly upon the door to the old man's soul, and crept in.

After an hour or two the old man stirred, rubbed his eyes with the backs of his hands, and woke from his sleep with a weight of sorrow in his soul. Despite his years the old man did not feel old, yet his dream had troubled him, and as he caught his reflection in the water he felt tears run down his face. 'I wish I had never been young,' he cried, as he brushed his wet cheeks, 'I could easily have borne being old if I had never been young, and my dreams tease me in the cruellest way. I am old, it is true,' wept the old man, 'and I have no heart for dreaming.'

He reclaimed his fallen hat from the dust of the river bank and watched as a butterfly opened and closed its wings on the felted head of a bulrush. 'I shall not come here to fish again,' said the old man as he carefully replaced the hat upon a dishevelled shock of silver hair; 'I have caught a fish which I can not throw back and I am haunted by its sorrow,' he sighed, as he closed the door to his soul.

The old man left the river bank much earlier than usual and walked slowly home through the forest, stopping every so often to listen to the song of a bird, or to look up at the trees. When he

48

arrived at his cedar-boughed shack he was tired again, but was afraid to sleep. He stretched his frail and ancient frame over an old mattress and stared at the log wall above him. 'A wise man does not look for what he knows he can not find' he sighed, as he slowly closed his eyes.

The day was not yet over, and the old man knew that he would be asleep by nightfall. But, as he closed his eyes, he vowed that when he returned to the forest he would try to forget that he had been there before.

On the distant river bank bulrushes whispered mysterious, unheard in evening breezes and, somewhere deep in the old man's soul, a small boy searched for butterflies.

Chris Tutton

THE COUNT

All gifts of beauty now departed
In sand eyed lamplit bareknuckled bend of day
Childless uncomfortable pillowed on the bell
Losing the count of magpie memories
A familiar stranger unready for the ring.

Chris Tutton

YULETIDE

Here's something I remember, grandmother;
your old house wrapped snug by the little walled garden,
the coal fire breathlessly hot and pine needles from the
Christmas tree embroidering the waxed wood floor,
the scent of pine and lavender a homely incense,
the old gilt-painted glass baubles worn and friable.

There were tangerines like clotted sunshine gleaming
in a blue glass bowl you'd brought back from Germany
and a little enamelled box studded with amethysts from Cairo
standing on the side table next to the silver-framed
photographs of your soldier husband and your
fair haired son in his smart RAF uniform.

I sat in your lap and played with your spun-glass beads,
each one a little universe of gleaming emerald;
you sang a song, half in Welsh, half in English
about home, and mothers calling their children
and under the drawn shutter of your eye
the tears slid like mercury for your lost men.

Here's something I remember, grandmother;
Winter's dark brings long remembering
and those who have passed are never gone from us;
the dazzle of lights and the tinsel wreath
hold in their sweet and foolish glitter
a dearer memorial than cold stone ever could.

Joolz Denby

FRUIT IN FEBRUARY

My mother dead. What did she leave?
Dry days of frost, a weight to grieve,
The dead wake us with worries,
Sour milk, the universe.

The hedge beneath the house was thick
With fruit, which gave the glow of milk,
The child's dream. She snatched fingers,
Mother's nightmare: "Pois-on-ous."

Birth, death, we sleep from dream to dream.
Beside my path to work, a gleam;
The same bush; the shadowed house,
Though birds shout, traffic murmers.

No, these small globes are not pure light
But crazed with brown. Flaws hurt her sight.
The dead leave us their worries,
White fruit for birds, snowberries.

Alison Brackenbury

THE FALL OF TROY

Before it became dark we watched rabbits
Trickle down the hillside like spring water,
Wild geese fleck mandarin suns
Spilling amber into the chenille of our shadow.
Before it became dark we fashioned
Moments into memories
Which would become
Too difficult to hold.
Before it became dark we
Touched each other gently
When we walked
Arm in arm like
Barge mules inching the towpath.

Chris Tutton

ANDALUSIA

The great cliffs of El Tajo fall in faded-velvet folds of ochre
to the thick embroidery of the plains below;
a horseman rides towards La Indiana in a whirl of
glittering dust; evening, veiled in the tattered drapery of
Heaven-blue and deep shadow purple, hides the day's
heat and a parched velocity turning in measures that saw

fields of sunflowers bleaching under the excoriation of noon
wither in stately rows like old duchesses wrapped in leaf-rags
grey as dirt, their echoing hands rattling with seeds.
Nothing human moves; the tongue of a lizard flicks heat,
olive trees twist patiently under their burden, hiding the silver
of their secret leaves that speak only to God.

Waiting for the paseo; caged verandas clasp blistered walls,
the ghost of a girl, high comb raising the mantilla whose lace
echoes the coiling petrified pattern of her iron prison.
Beneath, a boy strains for a glimpse of an almond-pale hand
that never sees the light: a crimson rose falling from soft fingers
heavy with bloody jewels – he weeps from the pleasure of pain.

Death dances with the maiden in an exhalation of night jasmine,
their embrace a longed for transgression wick with passion;
the dancer stamps her foot, her graven heel treads on the serpent's
                                                            head
as the Mother Of God gazes with ineffable tenderness from her
niche by the cathedral gate – calligraphy on the tiles shrouding
Her call Her by another name; but She is still a Holy Queen.

Silent, silent, the darkness flows heavy as old brocades
wrapping the sleeping town breathless in dreams of fire and
the battles of the red earth's savage past; a child frets, feverish,
the spectral troop rides on bone-rack steeds down
towards the river; Christian and Moor, it doesn't matter – all are
one now in the immeasurable beauty of Times's long sweet kiss.

Joolz Denby

NO DAYS OF GRACE

There are no days of Grace, no slow ascent to clarity
in the long surrender of Autumn into the white embrace of Winter.
Where do we fall in the vast undying gold of sunsets
out beyond the breath of sorrow or the glass splinter of ruin?

There are no days of Grace, no tatter-black rose unfolding
velvet in the night, rimed with frost's crushed diamond glitter.
How do we know what love can be when the thick blood
pulsing through us carries the fulminating virus of our cruelty?

There are no days of Grace but there are glimpses, fleeting, skewed
by the gelid distortion of the day's race and the flutter of life.
And we will be uplifted by those bright fragments into something
greater than our little selves, and know ourselves for what we are.

No days of Grace, perhaps; but shattered minutes of pure and
brilliant exultation in the long trek towards the last embrace.

Joolz Denby

THE LONG DAY HAS FALLEN

The long day has fallen to the horizon,
A lame nag arrowed in the homeward canter.
The moribund quarry grotesque in its capitulation,
A bloody mount struck riderless into the scar.

(Disingenuous sightseers gawp vulgar at the
Pre-carved spectacle of the withering mundane,
Stand awestruck by their inability to dog ear the page.
Caught between the sentence and the meaning
They punctuate the passage with grunts of ignorance.)

The long day has fallen to the horizon,
Fettered by loss to the stain of disgrace.
Urchins huddle chilled beneath a storm petrel sky
Where a whip crack moonless wind blows their
Seedless husk chalk dust fledgling footprints
Into the Christ hungry dark.

Chris Tutton

THE MOVEABLE ISLAND

…shifts, like the hull of a boat
left drifting, grounded on a different shoal
        each morning, in the midway, out
        where the Severn is letting, has let,
itself go into sea, like a thought into sleep:
        now you're there, now you're not.
        Today the outlook's vague, the weather
iffy. *Precipitation within sight: good… Low,*
        losing identity… If God could *dither*
        here's how it would look: these grand
tides like a lesson in bad governance, all power, no
        fixed purpose. No wonder the island
keeps its distances. Its reticence. Whichever
shore you look from, it seems closer to the other.

It's an abiding absence: in some
lights, a prison hulk; or, grey mornings after
        the storm, a lighthouse stump;
        a tanker, *stricken* (as they say, as if
the load that leaked, to blight our foreshores,
        was heart's-blood or grief).
        Sometimes it wallows, half
submerged, King Log hauled to and fro in state
        twice a day – a life or afterlife
        beyond us, though you can almost
see a way at lowest tides from shoal to shoal
        stitched with bird-tracks where a soul
not weighted by its body might – but for one last
narrow channel between – might just pass.

And now I'm closer, in the narrow
focus of my father's old field-glasses, adrift
on a plain of brown wave-furrows
till there: a skirt of mud-rock, un-
approachable by any craft, steepens to a paler grey,
with lichen blotches, then green
above the tide-line, grass, almost
wind-dried, salt-pickled, enough for a castaway
goat. A self-sufficiency. Or so
his binoculars say, though what
do they know – army surplus before I was born,
discharged from the ranks maybe
for just such imaginings: seeing a place that is not
for owning, most there only when you look away?

Philip Gross

THE SONG OF THE SHREDDER

is a gentle plangent wheeze. The page
creaks out, combed hard, like the edge of a weir,

arthritic water. Whiter than before, its shreds
want to re-knit – of its bones are coral made,

beached, bleach-dried… and peppered with mites,
ant-teams of crawling letters. It's an afterlife

of sorts: for a moment it flowers again

until page on page crams in, impacting to a tangle,
like twine in a drawer in a shed, a nest for something

rarely known to raise its young, or to be seen, or be.
Don't grieve for the text, released back into molecules

and bits for recollection, like us. Oh, but the song
at the moment of throughput: *eheu, farewell self, ah me.*

Philip Gross

YOUR DREAM, JOHN...
for John Duffy

It was North. It had hills. And me, dead.
A girl once slapped me for an indiscreet
sly moment in her last night's dream.
Was I touched? I could never decide.

But I'll attend now, for the inquest –
the highest and emptiest pub in the county,
cold enough for a morgue, an upstairs room.
I'll identify the body; yes, it looks like me,

a climber, boots worn at the heel
like mine. Which mirror shaved this stray
reflection off me? And how many others
might there be? All these self-seeds,

our multitudes, whirling like sycamore keys
down into each other's lives and dreams,
meant to die. Now I'm weightless, now afraid
how far the breeze might scatter me.

I've dreamed of dying, too.
I was choosing the music; I'd agreed –
why, I couldn't recall. I was having a tuck taken in
in the skin of my ribcage just over the heart

and woke choking – tears not just for me
but for the seamstress I'd given the job
and for the way she did it – honestly,
with love. With love I'll start

unpicking now, but leave this part of me
with you, to put down roots, to grow
to a tangle of crow's twigs in the pass
and make a mite of shade where two

roads cross; two travellers might stop
to share the kind of Thermos tea
that only tastes good on a climb, one
much like you, one the image of me.

Philip Gross

SUNDAY MORNING

The Sunday morning bells
are clanging and clanking,
droning and echoing,
and somewhere a dog, a black
cocker spaniel is howling,
and my rotund grandmother
wants me to go to the shop,
before the crowd leaves Mass,
to buy her Woodbines and
Silvermints, and get myself
a Peggy's Leg, so as soon as
the bells die away, Bonzo
and I head up the road,
where his enemy, the goose
is waiting to charge out,
lunging at him, while I
kick at the jabbing neb
and shout, calling the dog
after me, as the farmer
stands in his door and laughs
till we cross to the other side
where the shop should be
but isn't, and the dog
has vanished, and the cash
in my hand is a different
currency, and hundreds of
houses, streets, squares are
all around me, so I run back
down, but the sea is gone,
then the bells start up again.

Matthew Sweeney

BALLAD OF THE HORSE AND WINE

A horse neighed a loud hello
    as I went by with wine.
He did it to let me know
    he wanted what was mine,
but I ignored him, walked on
    with my half-case.
His neighs followed me down
    to the castly place
I was bivouacked in, with others,
    a ragtaggle bunch
of fathers, daughters, mothers,
    all eating lunch
when I carried my stash in,
    and one fellow got up
to snatch a bottle of the wine.
    Another grabbed a cup,
and filled it to the very brim.
    Before the rest could start
I retreated to my room,
    and imagine my heart
when I saw the horse's head
    through the window glass
and heard how he neighed
    and would not pass
so I hurried out to him
    to feed him wine,
whacking him on the bum
    as he glugged it down,

the others standing behind me,
    shaking their heads,
then stomping off loudly
    to take to their beds.

Matthew Sweeney

ON THE WAY TO POTSDAM

On the way to Potsdam I met a fox.
It was sitting in the corner of the S-Bahn carriage.
I looked around to see who its owner was –
every German has at least two dogs
so it made sense for someone to diversify.
No one was glancing at the fox, except me,
and it was me, only me, the fox was appraising.

Sure enough, when I got off at Potsdam
the fox immediately trotted after me.
I stopped, looked back, it stopped and stared.
Its eyes were brown pools of turf-water,
its face was a gypsy's who plays the guitar
so I walked on, knowing it would follow me,
and together we reached the Palace of Sanssouci.

Matthew Sweeney

DAY DREAMING

In a world where the sun rises for me, lights
peer from cracks in the roof
and a stag is spooked, paralysed by the concrete

spectre of a man, legless,
watching. Through glass, dark, in the distance,
I see a horse hung in mid-air;

one of many figures arrested, caught living, but gone
still – stiff as the dead: a bird
floating above a pear-like flame, a midget cornered

in pastel, four elements
in gold frames. Echoes multiply and fade, marking
my passage, reminiscent

of the sound in the black-and-white tiled hall where
my hesitant steps first
marked a slow entry into independence, the hard

cell of responsibility –
Achimota School. Here I learned the components
of light, the taste of fear,

sculpture's stiff pride, the chemistry of paint,
and I found a bright sun
doesn't always mean a good day for dreaming.

Nii Ayikwei Parkes

BY YOURSELF, BOY…

Q1

The basketball games I used to watch were
taped from a scrambled channel, had no sound
to speak of. I used to replay them in my head,
lend my own fillip to the images, splice them

into details: a hand like the arc of a mother's
belly awaiting the return of a ball sent down
to concrete; a half-raised foot – pre-fake and swivel;
a fall, fluid and dramatic, alive with the sweat

of exertion. For me, the moves had no names
but there were patterns in the chaos; determination
flexed hard on five faces usually muscled a win.

Q2

Those games had a silent energy that hung over
me, left clouds in my head that school could not
disperse. Walking past the main court for my piano
lessons, I would stop, listen to the older boys bragging,

belittling each other as they contorted their bodies
into screens of guile. I only went four times before
I skipped my first lesson – enough time for me to learn
scales, how to hold my hand above the keys, curved

like a basketball, but not enough to play anything

but *do re mi* and the bass lines of hit songs I'd heard
at the time. It seemed like music had lost the battle.

Q3

I learnt the language of the court: how to bow
low to breeze beyond the barriers of the zone,
crack my opponents by calling them names, advising
them to go home, spend some time alone learning

the rudiments of the game. This became my music –
the trash talk notated with polyrhythms of bounce,
the *oohs* and *ahhs,* the slick refrain of a swish shot.
I saw no connection between my new world and the one

I had deserted – the high post of the piano's back
the timed tap of feet, the bounce of hammers responding
to fingers and wires – until nineteen years later.

Q4

Nat King Cole's on the TV staring hard at his audience,
his hands setting up plays while he sings. Ray Charles
said he sang so damn well people forgot how good he was
on keys, and I see it now: his right hand stuffs a melody

down the grand piano's throat – that's the fake – he dribbles
the sound down to low notes until you expect the left hand
to come in lower. That's when he breaks mould, hustles
his left hand over the right throws high notes into your ear

-crossover, up, swish. Now the trash talk *it's better to be by yourself boy...* He smiles like the silent men on my tapes and, suddenly, every move has a name, a sound, a history.

Nii Ayikwei Parkes

A WHINE BEFORE SLEEPING

Right now I could use some red wine, a glass;
maybe a place to sit? And could I beg
for the sunset past? Just for as long as
it takes to drain the glass; so that the dregs
will be gorged by the horizon's ferment.
In fact, seeing as you can rewind time,
take me two sunsets back, to the moment
when my lover sighed beside me, her spine...

No, wait; thinking about it, I want none
of that – no reversals – just a promise
that tomorrow will come with time for fun –
won't be one of those finespun joys I miss,
a trickling red line on the horizon,
like the last file of wine, slight as a fin.

Nii Ayikwei Parkes

STREAM OF THOUGHT

Stream of thoughts flow out of reach
That washed this form up on this beach
Drowned, drenched, all life leeched
And dumped here on the sand.
So fair these limbs once, now chilled;
All movement's grace so stilled,
Bedraggled, limp, hair tangled filled
With this river's weed.

How came she here?
How comes she there?
Where estuary touches ocean's strand
And heedless of the wind.
Lost to the wicked waters, grim,
Dragged down by Peg Powler's fancy whim…
The mermaid who forgot to swim
Left lifeless on this ground.

And what a waste it seems to me
To take this life,
Or do I slag the river hag
Unfairly and unfound.
For drowned is all I certain know,
The truth shimmering behind a shroud.
The circumstance fair lost beneath
The ripples and the clouds.

Philip Coker

DREAM AWAY

It rained all day,
washed away the windows' grimey look.
From an attic flat
we saw the flash of thunder roll o'er Bournbrook.

And we only meant to take tea,
cups and saucers placed so....storm in a teacup, really.
Until the indica leaf saxophone echoed from the Wood,
and the Miles and Miles and Miles of drums
set the Winwood clouds in flood.

Somewhere between ocean and source....evaporation.
Somewhere between spring and sea....recirculation.
Somewhere between, amid, among,
the song already had begun to drift out on the tide.
Tiny drops of pewter plip-plop into turquoise pools,
splitting the sunlit surface into a thousand rippling
                                                    jewels,
where we can dive beneath the swell of mundanity
                                                    and rule.

Ssshh, ssshh, such a *rare device,*
steaming silver in these *caves of ice.*

Can you – you hear the roar of waves,
surging shoreward then sweeping out again?
Not to die
not to die but be reborn instead,
the Spanish castles' magic is straight ahead.

Stars like five hundred million bells;
the bells de St Exuprey they said,
the thing that is important is the thing that
                                        is not seen,
and so we slip into the drift of Spanish castle dreams.

Can you – you hear the roar of waves?
Breaking in and breaking out again.
Do you – you feel a little strange?
Are you here, or is it merely your body that remains?
Body from soul to the colours of sound and rhythm,
the subway base,
the outer star into electric blue………..a vision.

Looking east from Essaouira
Jubajima desert sand
is 'is sources blanc et bleu?
Imijination 'ubian.

Hear the voice of Ulmo
                    - estuary of Sirion –
Where the river meets the sea
                    - Neptune's dominion
Where the *interchanging melodies, woven harmony*
                                        and song
*pass beyond our hearing……*and are gone.
He said; *the sons of men will harken* then *unsatedly,*
(all else will be forgot)
for *the voice of the sea* shall call them
to *long for they know not what!*

So from the shore we waved.
You waved back....or so it seemed,
as the fair isle in the west flowed by
in the *big sea of our dreams.*

You were always so far out
and we were always waving;
where *the wind blows water white and black,*
where the mermaids syncobathing.

Can you – you hear the roar of the waves,
rolling onto, then rolling out again.
Can you – you hear the gulls' harsh cry.
Storm clouds gather before they thunder by.
I can hear it
   hear it
   hear it – the roaring of the pain.
The seagulls quark, quark, quark above the waves
lunar aspects leap
leap upon the tides,
magnesium flashes light up the sky,
as you take that last great dive
into the fathoms deep.

Ssshhssh! Ssshhssh!
Come come now listen close,
for when time turns to deuterium
he turns as light as helium;
Electric Lady.......ghost.

For *when you're dead you're made,*

he said,
you're made he said *for life.*
And so he slipped
beneath the drift
and passed far out of sight.

Philip Coker

KOCHEL 622

Yes. I see why he preferred the clarinet,
As my mother hunches, eyes closed, yet
Intent on tapes for her own funeral.

The clarinet is darker. Mud and oil
Have touched it; how he died, sick in a bowl;
Morphine; the steady heating of the seas,
Pale silk unwrinkled by a plump girl's knees,
The plunging horse, loose in a winter field,
The white perfumes a ripe lychee will yield,
Long nights. Dull days. The goldfinch and the hawk,
The dance of breath which washes out our talk
Spin on the wind. Above the tug of root

Yes, I know why I still prefer the flute.

Alison Brackenbury

ON A FEBRUARY NIGHT

When I dream of my mother, she is a voice.
Which is, I suppose, how we first know our mothers
In those forgotten waters. Women often talk too much.
Watch those who are quiet; they may be the ones
Who break a life, then smile. I am still whole.
But as I hear my mother, in the dream's dull room
Something slips then flutters, liquid as her lilt,
Tilts level with the air. It is a bat.
"Look, look," I say, but dreaming, no one sees.

Bats slept in the tall house, the one she loved,
In sash cords' gaps. My sister hated them.
My father drove them out. Look how they rise,
In clouds of voices, leaf for winter trees.

Alison Brackenbury

KEPT

In the orchid house it is still, quiet, warm.
There is no need to whisper or to shout,
To smudge your name on misted glass, stare out,
For staff, with spray and key, keep out all harm.

Slip off the crazed strength (which is your hope) like shoes,
This hot house whispers carpet on each floor.
Moss muffles senses. Wander on, adore
Blooms crammed on trestles, where no draught may bruise

Each orchid's trembled lip, ears which pulse green silk,
A violet mouth to let a bluebell fade,
Tawny a tiger's narrowed pupil made.
Heat stuns. We wander, children soft with milk.

How you once longed for this: love in ordered place,
The watchful clocks, the men who pad and pass
So gently, humming, polishing the glass.
Could you have flowered with them, tall unfreckled grace?

The storm blows huge. All branches bend to show
Its force. The green wood splits. Light leaves are hurled,
The trees ride out to battered dawn, a world
Deflowered, unloved, where you and I must go.

Alison Brackenbury

THE POND

I try to understand dark fathoms
of your fear, as when a child of yours,
not your only child, slid out of the womb
into unsounded water, failed to emerge into light
when your twins were born. You sang
their birth and wept that loss. Sorrow
deepest as you held and stroked that nameless.
Each pore felt the nothing slip away.

Each pond's green rim holds the solemnity
of unbroken waiting. You distrust mermaids,
the quick-finned, opalescent women who rescue
fabled mariner or baby from a downward spiral.
You understand, above that ancient mouth,
the sun-darkened surface never trembles.

Paul Sutherland

THE DESERTER

Above bold, whirring wheels
I cling to my window outlook –
with no desire to return, wanting
to push beyond journey's end
out into ultramontane regions
formed from twisting ravines
far from the world's call to arms.

In the night bucking double-decker
at the stormy front window in the upper saloon
an old soldier,
eyes blotto and limpid,
snatches my attention
I was in
the Black Watch…
He shouts above the roar.
Spit straight
straight in an officer's face;
not bearing his insult.
Zzip ,zzip, zzip,
off came the stripes,
zzip, zzip…
down on the ground.

My father,
in his country's uniform,
tried to make his return journey.
A fortnight he and his civilian friend
reached The Railway Tavern

for a farewell drink, then exhausted hours
with humour and reckless story-telling;
each evening they'd shamble back
to his friend's incredulous wife,
before in the morning, first thing,
he set out lucid once more to return.

I'm stretched, this journey,
further and further:
what prevails beyond arrival,
in mountainous interiors
at the end of maverick valleys
where retreat and extreme hubris
are at home: when anticipation of return hits
its vanishing-point?

My father didn't leave the war
with stripes on his khaki arms.

I visualise them
fluttering round his black buffed boots
as stretched ochre wings.

Paul Sutherland

THE DIVER

Perpendicular to the sheer cliff:
her caressing fingers ease around
pale ears, coax across the nape;
she guides and tucks her curls
until each haphazard glimmer's
hidden beneath her bathing-cap.
Streamlined, she flexes, raising
her heels and bracing spread toes,
springs from the bony platform –
four billion stars in a diver's arc
- almost a soundless entry-
stroke for stroke sets out to sea.

Paul Sutherland

THE WAITING ROOM

Unused seats crowd
the lit-up waiting room
bolted against
a stranded traveller.

Along the platform
under notices
latticed benches repeat.

Is it a disembodied breath
rocking the hinged sign?

In the dark flat pit
the double rails
turn to rust.

A slender-bodied
signal light
stands fixated on green
burns into the distance
mocking my late journeys

When youth's loneliness
seemed exhilarating: whole
metropolises flickered by
without one waving hand's
encouragement or welcome.

Where was I going:
to a fragrant lover's bedroom
that night?
who afterwards
fastened her door hard
against imagining travellers.

Did I jemmy open the front lock?

Through the ill-lit house
sneaked, bent over with doubt
ascending the stairs
tall with hope nudging ajar
the easily swung-open door:

she gleamed, from the window,
in her small corner bed,
as if never aroused
by a human hand.

Paul Sutherland

ALNMOUTH

Something unassuagable about an estuary.
Black ooze, oily,

Clinging. Dragging east,
Miles of cloud rubble.

Acres of sea-purslane.
Redshank, dunlin,

Camouflaged. Dissemblance.
Chains of footprints

Snaking through mud. Loops
Of old rope. A curlew

Letting go its rinsed notes.
Abandonment.

And, slowly filling with water,
A boat

Rotten beyond rescue, its anchor-chain
Stiff; paint, lichen,

Flaking from its timbers, revealing
Strong, clear lines. What matters

Is sunk, uncovered
And sunk. On the far bank, a train,

A straight line on the heugh,
Hauling its troubles south.

And between them, the river
Slipping from green fields, Scots pines, gables –

Pink, blue, terracotta –
From the gull-squabble,

Towards something sparer:

Wormcasts.
Ripples.

On the far side of the water,

Walls, roofless.
Gleaming bent grass.

Its surface wind-hatched, stippled with light,
The river

Is letting go
At the end of its life, an old man

Catching sight of what matters –
That muffled roar,

The stern white line of the breakers.

Katrina Porteous

NORTHLANDS
Commissioned by Yorkshire Forward

It is all about light here, the breathing light,
light that floods across the folded velvet swell of moorlands,
grazes the peaks, gilds snow and glimmers in the deep tarns.
It sets hawks dancing on the warm rising air
and shivers the faded desiccated bells of heather
that chime layer upon layer of flickering songs
about faith and love and the ancient, open North.
These crag-knotted, sky-blessed lands roll in clear
and savage majesty from coast to coast
bounded by icy feral strands, buffeted by winds
that write spells in the powdery sand and spindrift-glaze
the silvery-grey stone quays that bind the tiered seaside towns.
It's all about the light here, the heart catches fire with it,
the spirit rises high and bright with it – Northern light,
like no other, healing to come home to, heartbreaking to leave.

That light comes to the great Northern cities too,
picking out the convoluted carving on amber stone
or terracotta and red brick, quickening the humming mazes
woven tight with people from everywhere on earth,
all wrapped in light, gazing up at the opal sun rising in pale
                                            splendour,
smelling the faint breath of nature drifting like wild incense
from the stepping fells that lie so close around the urban hives.
Light blooms amongst the electric hustle of city days
as the streets stir from their brief sleep,
shaking off the theatres' hush and gesture, the glittering
dance clubs' pulse-beat, the raw tribal shout of guitars,

and the laughter of girls, tinkling with sequins, a twist
of jewels shimmering in the searing glare of neon and
the voodoo energy of the night-time carnival's crazy whip and
                                                        whirl.

The light, that soft, cool morning kiss, brings families
chattering into the day, sees schools bursting into the bustle
and hum of youth's furious salty flight, workers filling up
                                                        factories,
offices, shops and markets with the chanting hymns of daily life.
And in the pools of warmth caught on park benches, it smoothes
old faces, beautiful with memories, and smiles at babies,
stuttering on unsteady legs, peering in fresh wonder
at the complex brand-new enormity of grass blades.

The light is always, always with us in this huge and bone-strong
land and we are illuminated by its grace and exultant purity.
It shows us we can be anything; we can be everything;
we can make our own mythologies and our own futures,
we can be re-made by our passion and our dreams.

Every day light floods the Northlands;
every day the light,
every day the light,
that pure, fine and tempered light,
is with us.

Joolz Denby

VISTA

From here the view extends to nightfall.
Curious ramblers saunter tracing
These worn tracts of hollow earth
Like ancient arms
Weary of stretching for beauty.

Chris Tutton

I DEPARTED THE FETID HOUSE OF MY FATHERS WHEN EVEN THE FAWNING STENCH COULD NOT PERSUADE THEM TO CHANGE THEIR NAME

I returned with gifts of anger to the foot of the stoop of your
indifference,
Swept still with the wallowing wind of my repeated descent.
Crushed by a landslide of restlessness, scuttled by the
realisation
That I was always leaving. Forever shelling
Overmannered tributes to the shadowing dead from the
Pockmarked furrow of another nightscarred farewell;
Bruised by the fist of solitude,
Stained by the festering belly of a virgin moon
Falling crippled beneath the open window of its wound.

Chris Tutton

87

HARBOUR DAYS (A Salty Mosaic)

Trawlers brook spent like catches
Beached on sun bleached fenders
Where habitual partners perch dockside
Silent strangers to love. Swallows weave
And children unchecked by possibilities
Bind threads of imagination blind to the
Coarse and half spun fabric of their garb.
Radio incidental counterpoint orchestrates
Conversational preludes. Occasional invitations parade,
While the bayed racket of scavengers circling
Greedy for the spill fills the overmantle grey, where
Old men who can not rig the meter of their jaunt
Chew another windswept cured step toothless
From their Monday morning mile.

Chris Tutton

IN PRAISE OF DESPAIR

You were the wanderer
In my scorched and
Starburned night.
Gathering the lily,
Painting the
Scented notes of
Heartbreak for
The songs of
Imagined angels.

Chris Tutton

88

DOWN TO THE RIVER

Wanted to tell how light lay on the water

like panes of glass –
freckled with water-boatmen and mosquitoes –

On the oily, braided river
moving through oak-woods
with narrative grandeur

it was glass afloat like sails –

Light composed texture after texture –
gleams that could have been the smooth pelt
of shape-shifters,
reflections in the glazed terrace
of a waterside café:
                    To step through, or not?

Our faces were younger then, malleable.

Do you remember dazzle,
I should have asked,
Doors of light appearing in the river
as if we could step in
to a second life –

                    that last time,
we reminisced the way old lovers do

before a death –

How was it that evening seemed full of glare;
shuffled, new?

Fiona Sampson

SUN STREET

The tree fills with light.
A perfectly ordinary pear – blind, too, this year –
in a side-garden in a side-street
in a leafy suburb of Vilnius,

its sun-filled foliage crowds the window
and somehow seems extraordinary –
the pale full leaves, trembling a little,
turn to the sun yet tip away.

Beyond the tree,
as if among its branches,
workmen are building a terrace.
Tak-tak, go their mallets. Knocking on wood.

Fiona Sampson

ARS POETICA
for A.J.

Every elegy a love-poem; every love-poem
a kind of elegy. You live between
closeness and loss, fear and reward,
and look up to both as if to parents –
they knew what you were even before
you knew it yourself.
                              Then seemed to relent,
on the secret logic of whim:

till you turn and see each again,
waiting it out in the summer garden, where trees
fan green plumage over gravelled walks,
implying – footsteps. Or they'll shift, like breezes,
round the open window where you talk
on your cell-phone to this month's lover:
See, they say. It goes on. It's never over.

Fiona Sampson

POST-MARKET

Pomegranates explode.
Figs, flesh bursting.
Grapes bleeding.
Melons, under the knife.
Apples chopped
and coconuts smashed.
Bananas, skin peeled.

Garlic crushed.
Olives stoned.
Black-eyed beans.
Tomatoes squashed,
black and blue aubergines.
Potatoes dust themselves and rub
bruised courgettes
with dandelions.
Ladyfingers stroke
onions full of tears.

Thyme scented honey,
olive oil mixed with oregano;
potions.

Kostas Hrisos

ZEMPEKIKO

It's so much more difficult to learn
a dance that has no steps.

A single note from a
three-string bouzouki
echoes
from its long neck in
its round belly
resonates
in the hollows of
the heart,
stirs the nerves.

Knees bent, as if he's praying.
Fists clenched, as if he's cursing.
Feet stamp the earth, as if it's her fault.
Arms outstretched; ready to take flight
                                        Free.

Kostas Hrisos

Zempekiko: a Greek dance
Bouzouki: a Greek musical instrument

ECOLOGIC

When the Earth was put in our care
Such a delicate thing
It was wrapped in bubble wrap
Which we keep bursting
Because it relaxes us

Kostas Hrisos

THE HIGH-RISE FLATS

They are knocking down the flats
by the coast road.

Ordinary lives
still echoing around
on a blue wallpaper strip
of the child's bedroom,
on gaping kitchen drawers,
muffled by the abandoned sofa.

From a broken window
on the ground floor
a dirty red curtain is flapping
defiantly:
the cape of the matador
inciting the bulldozer.

Kostas Hrisos

BLUE TELESCOPE

In my last dream my hair was blue,
my head was a Roman bust.
I woke up and tried out my voice –
I heard the harsh tone of a parrot.
What could have caused this change,
this backward-look through a telescope?

I once owned a miniature telescope –
it was, as I recall, the same blue
as Chelsea's. I hope they never change.
Anyway, it's long since bust.
I'd point it at the neighbour's parrot,
opposite, while mimicking its voice.

People tell me I have a good voice
with some of the qualities of a telescope.
Think of the sudden shriek of a parrot,
the leap into the eye of the sea's blue
as you focus. Or an engine's combust-
ion. Or any other abrupt change.

You know, I try to stop all change.
Might as well wish for a woman's voice
or even better, a woman's bust.
I once banished the telescope,
and as it was carried out, blew
through a trombone, like a parrot.

I've never wanted my own parrot,
even though it would make a change
to living alone, between those blue
walls, having only my own voice.
I may search for a parrot bust
to peer at, daily, through a telescope.

There's a timelessness about a telescope.
The same can be said about a parrot.
I imagine a huge sculpture of bust
telescopes, dead parrots, in an exchange
for eternity, with a parrot's voice
on a loop, and the whole painted blue.

It was all visible in my blue telescope.
Games of Poker, change or bust.
The only voice the cry of the parrot.

Matthew Sweeney

TO ASH AGAIN

The urn turned upside down,
emptied out the ashes
and rolled away. The wind
grabbed each ash flake,
swooped it into the sky,
swirled it across the sea,
over fish, through gulls,
and on the other side
the ashes came together
to form the reborn man
who stole a bicycle,
pedalled up a mountain
and into a rushy tarn
where he drowned,
while the urn floated
across that same sea,
rolled across sand, fields,
then up that mountain, as trout
heaved the corpse out,
lightning bolts blasted it
to ash, which the urn ate,
then turned upside down...

Matthew Sweeney

WINDMILL STEADS

Even after they left,
When strangers ripped the stones from its old walls, burned

Its roof-tree, oak
Stripped from a shipwreck, raised

Outside new, shiny sea-front homes,
Revetments for the sea to thump against,

What remained of its rooms –
Turned inside out, crowded with sour nettles –
Hissed

Back at the white rigs, rip-tides, where
On east wind nights, the sea beat at the door,

The cradle rocked like a boat in the swell's back-draught.

Herring
Came and went. Houses.

Then the old ones, helpless,

Mouthed one last prayer against
The sea's indifference.

Katrina Porteous

HOLY ISLAND ARCH

Against the buffeting wind and the sea's growl
The crafted stone
Soars overhead in the high blue forever,
Thin as a wishbone.

Nothing so fragile should stand so strong.
Leaping, unbound,
As if quarried blocks were weightless; as if wind
Could not suddenly dash them down,

The sandstone balanced by the mason's hand
Impossibly, holds.
All grace defies weight, logic, weather –
Bends like a bow,

Hope, launching itself
Into cold space.
The breaking sun transfigures it. An equal,
Opposite embrace

Is all that keeps the stones from crashing,
And the heart,
That has one longing only – to be met and held
In such an arch.

Katrina Porteous

SHANKY

Shanky is all England:
A barn-conversion.
Strangers in four-by-fours. Forgotten

Names: the Butty Meadow. Shanky Hall.
The nugget of a chapel.
Faith in ruins.

Down the Long Nanny Burn
A green gate leans.
Dark, witchy hawthorns

Point along the leat
To Shanky Mill,
Its bricked-up windows, walls

Empty, its rafters open
To the swifts, the rain;
The knotted fabric of the farm

Shrunk, first, to one man
Alone in his tractor cabin,
Radio on; then

To no one
But the nostalgic, who like it here
At nightfall, when

Black cows wallow in the burn
And the low sun
Floods everything golden.

Katrina Porteous

THE FULMAR

I watch the fulmar hurl its breast
To the wind's unseen geometry;
Spread wings on nothing, reckless of gravity,
And ride that risk
And rest
On sheer uncertainty,

Choosing no choice.

I must learn to be like him,
To follow the reach and search of air –
Swoop, sink, stand, balance, soar on the invisible spiral stair –
And not resist
But trust,
And be carried there.

Katrina Porteous

CUT

The score is brooding down in the lower register
as she puts the children to bed; says *goodnight,
don't let the bedbugs bite.* Cut to her face
as she looks back from the door. The light
from the stairs throws shadows behind her
as she puts her hand to her mouth and blows another
slow kiss. Jump cut to her at the top of the staircase
held in silhouette. Slow the music ready for a fright.

Cut to him pacing up and down in the kitchen.
Then cut to a close up of the floor and slow
everything down while fading out the music
so only the soles of his shoes falling onto the lino
can be heard above him muttering in German.
Cut to him by the door as he stops to listen.
Bring back the music like a punch to the stomach.
He calls out her name *June;* again *June* – an echo.

Close-up of her eyes widening and cut straight back
on the next beat to his hand on the kitchen door
and on the next beat to the foot of the stairs
as his shadow is thrown out across the floor
and spills up the wall. Cut then to the shock
on her face and let the camera track
her down to the hall. This is when the hairs
on the necks of the audience rise with the score.

They know that in this scene what is going to happen
happens. This delicious terror is a very peculiar pleasure.
They fear for her and of course are on her side, but

would be disappointed if she survived. Cut from her
to the sleeping children to heighten the tension.
Don't let up, cut back to him so their pulses quicken.
They don't actually see it happening, but
they do hear the knife – clatter to the floor.

Martin Figura

TRIP TO THE ADMISSIONS WARD

The nurse puts a gentle hand into the small
of Frank's back, holds the other out, palm up
for him to take, whispers that he will lead.

The fluorescent lights blur as Frank is spun away
down the white corridor. The doors, full of grinning faces
flash past, the clapping gets faster and faster. The nurse's

keys crash against his hip like a tambourine. People
are shouting his name, slapping him on the back
as he passes. The ward is strung with bunting.

Frank sits dizzily on his bed to read all the cards,
while coloured balloons bob on ribbons
from the window bars. This is quite a welcome.

Martin Figura

THE BATH

Crow-eyed nurses watch the faint echo of a man
in six inches of bath water, silver-white lithium
drifts metallic through his blood stream. The span
of his hand in front of his face takes the low hum
from his mouth, returns it as a pebble to his tongue
for him to swallow, keep in the swim of his belly
below the muffled drum of his heart with all the rest.

Martin Figura

THE WEIGHT

He moves as if he were full of stones
and the room a river, numb cold shoving
against his legs. The crow-eyed nurses
want to know how much of him is left.
He feels a thumb under his jaw, is lifted.
Scales accept the load, its muscle, its breath,
its knuckle bones.

Martin Figura

Write about the happiest you've ever been. Alternatively,
write about the most frightened you've ever been.
(Natalie Goldberg)

In a back bedroom, in a back street
where the clickety clack of heels caught in the dark,
could not be heard that night.
Women with hair got up in brunette clouds
and their laughter, was all silence.
No street light or star or landing light
coming in under the gap of the door.
The arrangement of possessions
in the meeting of two walls, the difference of it.
The dark, flat sea above, the moonless depth of it.
Rigid in someone else's bed, heavy curtains, the gap,
the extra slice of night knifing into the room.

The ironing board like a plane's wing,
the doughy bulk of Nana, bent over it.
Like hovering mist, a drift of sixties cold air
under the sofa. Vosene shampoo in my heavy hair,
hair heavy as an animal on my shoulders.
Nighty flimsy, nightie white.
Feet, size one packets of ice, tucked under my bum.
The golden starburst clock crawls like a dying man.
Waiting for Mom.
Someone lets off a rocket, its blue sparks glitter
into the garden. Where's the celebration?

All the toddlers in their colours: skirts of orange,
cerulean dungarees, sludgy tights. Whirling

105

round: spinning, blending, spiking
like Damien Hirst had them on his turntable.
Blue leather shoes with bars, two podgy parcels
of white socked flesh, the fun of it, the daring of being Three.
Then you are gone into the colours,
in your dress of seashell. Blue cancels out pink,
orange cancels out white, everything cancels out Seashell.

A tumbling of yellow leaves beneath trees,
flourished like picnic blankets since last night's
frost. Where were you last night?
Not watching leaves fall, I'd bet my life.

Tom Cruise freezes mid grimace, mid-tough guy.
An arctic blast of frost across the screen –
the pilot, his consultant's tone soothes,
tells us to strap ourselves in, weather the storm.
Wind arrives from the edge of the universe,
all we can do is move forward into a chaos.
We are onlookers, miles up, tangled in weather
as if we strayed into occupied territory
where a battle rages in the dignified piazzas of the sky.

Roz Goddard

I WANT TO BE AN ANGEL

I give you this, a silver coin.
Keep it in your pocket
and know by touching it
you cannot be bad.
When you are sockless, without a coat
when your mother is drunk asleep in the afternoon
heavy curtains keeping out the sun
when your father creases the living room door,
touch the coin.
When you are left at school with the cleaners
when you count stars on the long walk home
when plaster from the slamming door
falls on your head, gentle as snow
when your bike is sold
when you pray for silence
when you land in your seventh town
with its unfamiliar trams and roofs of northern rain,
touch the coin.
Remember what I said
that soft crayon-smelling afternoon
the two of us bent over the extraordinary words
you had written.
Remember what I told you.

Roz Goddard

TIMES WHEN I DREAM

You arrived. The hills were as they had ever been.
Trees marched up the contours of the land, hiding clearings,
stories in moss.
After a barely warm day, the sun was a fragile coin of Honesty
clouds had been driven off, pushed to the edges of the sky
what remained was a dance floor, huge and blue.

Down the valley two dogs answered each other. The weather vane,
a crow, creaked to the West, then was still.
In the oven a lasagne came alive – a bubble of layers mixing cream
                                                                  and blood
a few stars disintegrated, fell to the table. In the dregs of my glass, a
                                                                  forecast.
I had expected simply to enjoy the wine, a meal, some talk about
                                                                  books.

Roz Goddard

AUNT FRIEDA'S VOICE

the train rattles off its full vocabulary
moving along its noise beside a line of nettles

we pass through the concrete bowl
where echoes play ball with my voice

in one of these blocks a disused sound,
an intimate richness,
waits to be hauled onto Austrian tracks

David Hendtlass

THE ABSENT

1

Beside a lane a garden roams unchecked:
its hedges lean against the clouds and scratch
the house, which from the hill is a mere pebble.

Roses have flocked, white butterflies, to watch
the dry proceedings of unhindered dust;
heaps of old journals yellow on a table.

In memory I enter these dear rooms:
the Sunday side, where vase and mirror curve;
the older, darker half, where three trees shake.

I lift the low latch, glide into the gloom:
the boiler mutters and the bath tub leers;
large, metal taps reach for my hands and grip.

2

The house is dressed
in polished rain and sleet,
its pebble-dash
hard as orchard apples,
or the dry stair
where three aunts bent to climb
up to their ninetieth year.

A rose shines,
a baggy star
as I pass through whirring sparks of dark;
father's shaving brush
moulders, mournful.
Mum snores:
I listen.

At the end of the bed,
where hags crowd,
a fever crouches,
scorning amends.
My mother still remains:
fearful, I clutch.

3

First Voice: There are no visions here,
no deep incisions here,
though a certain air of misgiving
where we see by the glare of invisible gas
and dark hardens the larynx,
infiltrates the lungs.

Second Voice: I hear hot tongues probe rusting gutters
while we, secreted, daily feel darkness
pounce like a cat
scattering black feathers.

First Voice: I recollect this house
where together we grew apart
under childhood's magnifying eye:
the house was its own animus
(us it inhabits)
in its different conditions, its several storeys.

Second Voice: The sun rose on the front porch,
roses forced the back panes;
we veiled the diamond window,
slid the sliding door.

David Hendtlass

DAVID AND BATHSHEBA

Over bed-springs, armchairs and paraffin heaters
pan more slowly up the scarp of refuse
past plots of bath tubs sprouting bulbous taps
towards a dome of diamond blue:
wreckage of a Morris Minor.

Here David sits, lord of his domains:
incendiary brows raise his woollen cap,
his forehead pitted with notes as on a stave;
his look deflects a disused railway
cropped by nettles.

A magnolia hosts its Jewish candles
where she reclines, bathing in a rain-filled tub
                                                    :

her flesh reveals a perfect rhyme –
white as two swans
skimming a restful lake, adrift.

David Hendtlass

MEMORIES OF TRUFFAUT'S "LES QUATRE CENTS COUPS"

The teacher strides in black and white to the board,
scuffs chalk while writing signs percussively.
The boy behind the fourth desk is bored, glances fingers
over the magazine nude and hands it on with obligatory snigger
for his peers to snog and flick at ears. – Through the air a
white projectile raids the radar of ducking pupils:
the teacher's just a mouth enunciating rage,
his French so unlike Balzac's prose
which the boy has caught by heart and candle-vision.
Antoine lays his radiant story
on the table at the front, his makeshift altar,
recalling how his pencil landed to the cheers of a full-stop.

Next day the teacher summons him to the spot
where all eyes converge,
brands him thief, chief of insolence,
national traitor
to filch the words of France's mighty writer.
Antoine reels, his blush of shame detained forever
on black-and-white film.

The flat is long, almost a train with carriages.
His knife tastes the friction
with which his parents move their loathing on;
the candle, fallen for Balzac,
spills its alphabet of tongues,
emblazoning its worship on the cloth.

His mother crosses his low space in the dark,
light clicks on.
He's forgotten to take out the trash:

runs back up the stairs
and jumps at his shadow in cement.

He and his friend swear truancy
down streets injected with young air.
By the poster of some pouting starlet
he kisses his hand, hungrily.
His name is hammered into criminal files.

In a van
waltzing through city neon;
with ageing prostitutes he descends;
his cheek, tear-kissed,
turns
into light.

Breaking out, followed by shouts,
he bolts through hedges and fields,
runs on till water's edge
forces him to waver and tack

tracking rectangle

closing in

closes

fin

and the boy's face
turned on you and me
with that last, defiant, uncertain, look back.

David Hendtlass

SPEAKING OF BIRDS
for Jamie

'Heart...keep beating,
brave messenger, bearing news of yourself' (Ken Smith)

For weeks now I've been trying to recall that poem,
the one you spoke of: Saxon parable of that little bird,
maybe a sparrow, arrowing through rafters in a confusion
of light and rowdiness and noise, and then back out

into night; that brief spell of warmth between
two darknesses. I'd been reading you some Hughes –
the one about swifts, the memory of flight – across
electronic miles. Foolish. The hiatus as I realised

the words would coagulate into death.
                                        And it had come
and squeezed you, clenching your heart like a sparrow
(yes, again) in a hawk's embrace. There are some places
we can only tread alone.   But the raptor let you go –

these daily remissions, returns of seasons, cycles, tides.
So it is that your heart can perch again, perch,
brave messenger, on the wires; these complex tributaries
of messaging. Daily miracles – friendship, laughter, love –

against all odds of being here at all. So we sit across
the candles, speak of entropy and order in this

continuing present, this universe of the ten thousand
things. Beginnings and endings in each becoming moment.

We breathe it all in and out; wise enough now to recognise
the many shades of grey that make the rainbow.
The flow, decay, and flow again.
                              The candles, of course, burn
lower; but in the spiced air our laughter outshines the autumn dusk,

and the birds in our blood still fly towards the light.

Roselle Angwin

IN THE WOODS IN SCOTLAND ONE FEBRUARY
30 YEARS AGO READING YEATS

trying to tickle trout: pursuing that glimmer
no matter how cold the water, no matter
that they always eluded our hands, because

there was always the chance, a shimmer
at the horizon's cusp, that one day a belonging
might appear, might arch its back to our fingers

Roselle Angwin

116

DIAGNOSES
for my parents

i Alzheimer's

Once she found a goldcrest's nest,
tucked it carefully in a crook, made sure
the entrance was clear and open.

Recently the winds have blown it far
from the tree, are gently taking it apart.

ii Infarct

The last dominoes perch unsteadily.
The rest have fallen so that their black
sides are uppermost, the numbers
and the narrative mostly obscured.

Roselle Angwin

DUNSTANBURGH
(*Excerpt*)

An August night. Above the clouds
Over the Egyncleugh, the moon

Rises. The wind is slowing down,
The world relaxing into sleep.

Not a bird on the water. Only the hush
Of the long grass, and the sea's wash,

And the slightest stir of birds on the cliff –
A cleared throat, a chuckle, a cough:

A ship of sleepers cast adrift.
A crane-fly whirs. Papery moths,

Water-marked wings the colour of stone,
Drift through the thistles; and the moon,

Climbing, draws a path across
The darkening water; phosphorous

Catching the ripples as they run
In liquid silver, a seething shoal
Of scales and fire.

               The castle walls
Loom higher in the dark, a great
Wrecked ship. The moon illuminates

Its cargo – feathery grasses, lichens,
Spokes of hogweed, may-crown plantains,

Daisies, studding the decks like stars.
Its brightness calls, and all light things answer.

In the courtyard, around the foundations,
The kitchens, the chapel, the Constable's chambers,

Leathery wings flit. Woodlice trundle,
Armour on stone. A spider trembles,

A web's bull's-eye in the moon's full glare.
On the arc of its journey, fierce white fire

Catches and fills a heart-shaped window.

And the deepest dark of the castle walls –
Doors going nowhere, hearths, holes,

Garderobes, stairways bent at odd angles –
Join with the wider dark, the miles

Of field and heugh, and wind-blown fell,

Millennia of dark, the men
And women lost beyond recall,

Absorbed in silence, earth and stone.

Katrina Porteous

CUTTING THE POPULATION

I remember that day in the barber's
When Patrick's dad was there
He took something for the weekend
And left behind some hair,

And though I was of tender years
I knew for Roman Catholics
That something for the weekend
Should be church not prophylactics,

I sat and had my hair cut
And thought of Patrick's dad
And thought of Patrick's mother
And how much sex they had,

Was it just at weekends
When the pair would get it on?
And was it just at weekends
When half his hair had gone?

And then I thought of Patrick
And his brothers Phil and Steve
His sisters Jane and Catherine
Not forgetting Gill and Eve

It seemed that on most weekends
Patrick's dad was getting hot
And it didn't really matter
If his hair was cut or not.

Marvin Cheeseman

THE FRIDGE FREES YER

Escapism's essential
in a world that gets too loud
you can drown yourself in alcohol
with all the other crowd
some people play bingo
posher folk play bridge
me, I like to listen to my fridge

When all the noise is over
when all the day is done
I sit down in the kitchen
and hear its gentle hum
that reassuring resonance
that monotonal drone
that veritable vibrance
that murmered methadone

So don't be playing bingo
have a break from bridge
sit down in the kitchen
and chill out with the fridge.

Marvin Cheeseman

MYSTICAL MOTHER

My mate's Mystical Mother,
Used to live on a barge,
She told me she was a medium
But she looked like an extra large.

I remember we emptied a drawer once,
Where all her undies were put,
As we surveyed the scattered smalls,
I thought they were anything but.

My mate's Mystical Mother,
Was arrested, I forget the charge,
And when she escaped the papers said:
Beware there's a medium at large.

Marvin Cheeseman

FRIENDS

Sindy and Barbie
argued
neither's plastic
legs could
sit astride.

Their pinched waists
were made
for standing
in kitchens
modelling
evening gowns.

Sindy could
abseil
Barbie's golden
mane got hooked
on guttering.

To the rescue
ActionMan descends
on yellow wool
frayed
against
pebble-dashed
dreams –
Barbie amongst
the pansies.

Sindy galloping
to the rescue
lilac tutu
ripped on
scarlet rose bush
spying Barbie's
mud splashed
floral pinafore.

Sindy and Barbie
rifling through
ActionMan's
barracks
get away
undiscovered.

Barbie in khakis
beautiful locks shorn
Sindy in
bikini and boots
messengers
dispatched.

Maya Chowdhry

GRAFTING

our love was quiescent
her tongue cut my limps until I
was too pruned to last the first frost
I waned through winter
my rootstock reaching earthwards
bark peeling to mulch

all winter through dormant dreams
I thought about grafting myself
onto the body of her new love
imagined my cut limbs on
her torso frozen through solstice

after imbolc a tear growing in her skin
my arms sprouting out
to hold my ex-lover again

Maya Chowdhry

THE SKY WILL BE CLOSING IN 30 MINUTES

Can all clouds please collect their small fluffy ones
from the Sky Lark crèche.

Clouds must keep their misty outlines with them at all times,
unattended wisps of milky air will be treated as suspect
and destroyed by Mr Blue, head of Sky High Security Services.

Lavish yourself in *To The Skies:*
The largest supplier of clouds to be seen
above the line of sight.

Will a member of Sky Security please report to Mr Blue immediately!
Will a member of Sky Security please report to Mr Blue immediately!

Bargain-Cloud-Day:
Three clouds for the price of two on rainy Mondays.

The Sky's The Limit:
The biggest mass of apparent canopy over our heads
in the Universe.
Open 24 hours, 7 days a week.
Sky: for all your weather needs.

Will a member of Sky Security please report to Mr Blue immediately!
Will a member of Sky Security please report to Mr Blue immediately!

The sky will be closing in 5 minutes.
Please make your way to the nearest exit.

Maya Chowdhry

SUMMER CYCLE # 3, EARTH

I tread lightly because the earth is broken.
Lightly not out of choice, my legs won't reach
the ground. Fear of breaking it further
congeals in my quadriceps. I want to walk
on the ground, am sick of being air.

I tread lightly. The earth is full of memory.
To stand squarely on the ground is
to remember. It remakes the circuit,
the slamming static build-up will ground itself
in one blue arc. It stops the heart.

The electrical jolt fires the most important
of muscles. Nerves burn like a fuse box
in an old house. The box in the cellar
where we put away our clutter, where I
find ideas of ourselves after you've gone.

I tread lightly. I walk past where we used
to live. That part of town has closed its doors.
The earth's arms ready to take me when I fall
to her. The earth's weight ready to take
the best and the worst of us. The earth does not
forsake what was and what is. I tread lightly

throwing down salt to bleach the pavement.
Placing soil on the breast of the dead. Kicking
at the four posts that form the directions
to try to bring the sky down.

I tread lightly. Each step down begins
a journey they say. Each step down begins
a time-line. I see future histories
radiate from each step of connection,
they fly out in blue sparks; wishes, promises,
and time-lines. I would rather not know where
these paths lead. To just follow one like a tram line;
two rails and their sleepers, always the same
distance apart as they perspective to an horizon.

I flail my legs like a boy with too many balloons,
or a big golf umbrella caught in the wind. Reach
for the earth and repel from the earth. The earth
won't forget or let me sleep until I give her my weight.

John Siddique

GREEN DOGS

We lay melted in green light, stretched out like dogs in their total gift of themselves. My hand on her belly, so much so that we were both completely pregnant. The light seemed to come from the child and be both of us, and we were one moment, with the gentleness of dog kisses to heal a wound. We were like that. We were one day.

Each day is anchored into that harbour; words, faces, walks, work, are turned over and over in my hands. Each surface felt and checked, each corner, any mark. Arcing back in sex magic. Life spent trying to live one day. Parcels turned over and over inside oneself looking for jewelled light.

A night we lay, not able to sleep. We slipped into space beyond sleep, where microcosmic trembling lifts like some veil. Like dogs unravelled and unified with each other. A trinity that became without expectation.

John Siddique

THE GREEN WATER THAT IS NOT AIR

Last night in the depths where the iris flowers wait out the winter
in their bundle of roots the blue horse came and breathed at my
neck. Was it I who was lying with the roots in the silt of the pool?

My father was the best-ever diver, and I was so proud when he
climbed the cliffs higher than anyone, feet and feet above the sea,
and shaped a pointed crescent and fell out falling into the air.

This summer I dreamed a naked woman cradling a salmon too
big to fit into the bag at the airport. In J's dream he woke me
from my fishy one by calling out: *the little stream...* Next
morning in the hot gorge J and I stopped at the ruined monastery
at Marsiac, and there was my woman and fish engraved in
limestone, right beside the river.

Yes, it is me in the mud of the pool with the salmon and the iris,
and on the cliffs high, too high, above me my father is still
falling, falling through the green water that is not air.

Roselle Angwin

CLAUDE GLASS/WHAT THE POOL KNOWS

Despite the light crashing through fractured branches
the pool's ink meniscus is impenetrable, dark-skinned,
opaque as an ancient language I've forgotten how to read.
Everything's gathered to this locus, made unfamiliar.
The tracks at the brink give their secrets more openly:
spell out boar, deer, duck. The pool's spread exposed
on the hill's limestone bones like a sore, weeping out
over culled trunks and stumps. I saw a water snake last time,
you tell me; and I picture the glass cracked and fissured
in ripples and waves, veering between dark and light; consider
how sometimes the point of entry has to be by the wound.

Roselle Angwin

*A Claude Glass (or Black Mirror) is a small mirror used by artists,
slightly convex in shape, with a dark-tinted surface.*

THE INEVITABLE CATASTROPHE OF INTERPRET-
ATION BEGETS THE UNNATURAL BASTARD BIRTH
OF DISILLUSION

Wounded in crossfire reverie as the sun fell masquerading as
                                                            sleep.
Waking faithparched, shaken, breathless, to discover the
                                         bleating dreaming blind.
Invoking reassurance from solemn psalms of abbreviated
                                              glances,
Crouching in such shallow phrases our thoughts could not
Pose naked for the night.

Threading ritual-sophist spangle onto starsplit drapery of
                                             deception
Frostwoodsandaled, scalpel cold. Bluff-carved hunkering anxious
                                             beneath a
Cherry minted thirty pieces of browblood burnished silver moon
                                             swollen
Easeled between quivering aleamber thighs of impenetrable
                                             scars,
Painting the stray lambs of our whimpering shadows newborn
                                           soft,
Unkilned still by regret, cadaverous stains of arpeggiated
                                           evening pallor.

Chris Tutton

TRANSIT

A girl walks by, leaves the air thick
with the scent of cocoa butter; an *abuela*
places a half-drunk can of soda in her bag –

complete with straw – while smiling at her
granddaughter, a junkie scratches and talks
fast, believes he's still slick enough to lure

a woman with a quick flick of the comb
he keeps in the stretch of his socks.
I catch a whiff of nail varnish, spy

the balancing lean of a woman painting
her nails in the subway. Vanity is casual
and love, it seems, the cost of a wide smile

cast across the length or breadth of a carriage:
father to daughter, woman to man, stranger to
stranger, as the rumble moves from darkness

into the unknown void of another station.

Nii Ayikwei Parkes

FRESH ARGUMENT

For the dressing:
Tone, time and taunts

For the jambalaya:
Intolerance, indifference, resentment, and egos.

Preparation

1.
Take a sliver of tone and amplify it.
Sour it with vinegar and agitate.
Wait for five seconds while it settles
then throw in a sprinkle of subtle
taunts. Put the dressing to one side.

2.
Use a carving knife to slice
a bright circle of intolerance
and lay it at the base of a mixing
bowl. To season, throw in a fist
of indifference, then add a twist
of mouth and two litres of well-aged
resentment. Add two egos
and beat the mixture
until it is as smooth as spite.

3.
Pour the jambalaya into a black,
anger-lined pan and place it in an oven

preheated on the fires of a recent disagreement.
Let it sit until burned brittle.
Sprinkle it with fresh seeds of the sower.

4.
Serve the dish hot
with a dash of cold dressing.

Nii Ayikwei Parkes

TO THE BLACKSMITH

To the blacksmith who weighs the horse's whole history
                                                     between his knees,
Who cradles its foot like a gypsy reading a palm,
Carving its future in curved horn
With knife and nail and sizzling iron, I say:

Beat me a set of shoes to ease
Lameness of heart. On your black anvil, pound
Metal on metal till the swarf flies. Straighten me.
Make my way sound.

Katrina Porteous

THE QUESTION

The small boy wandered into a shady copse of doubt and
wrestled with problems he could not resolve. As he knelt down
to look more closely at an unusual flower, he suddenly noticed
that the flower had disappeared, and in its place he was surprised
to see a grey toad. He continued his descent onto the soft ground,
and was about to stroke the toad with an outstretched finger
when the toad immediately changed into a young lamb. Amazed
and delighted the small boy stroked the young lamb joyfully,
ruffling its soft, curly coat, until it let out a fearful roar and at
once changed into a bear. The small boy jumped to his feet in
terror.
'Don't be afraid,' said the bear.
'But you could harm me!' uttered the small boy nervously.
'I could indeed. And sometimes you will meet me and regret it.
But not today.'
'Who are you?' the small boy asked, almost too afraid to move.
'I am truth,' replied the bear, drawing himself up onto his hind
legs, looking twice as tall and even more fearsome.
'But you change so quickly and easily,' cried the small boy,
awed and shadowed by the bears' huge, upright frame, 'how
shall I know it is you if I meet you again?'
'That,' riddled the bear, changing into a cloud and floating away,
'is something that only your own questions will be able to
answer.'

Chris Tutton

BIOGRAPHIES

ROSELLE ANGWIN

Poet, author and painter Roselle Angwin is the director of Fire
in the Head creative and reflective writing programme. Her most
recent books are a poetry collection, *Looking For Icarus* and the
Arts Council supported *Writing the Bright Moment – inspiration
and guidance for writers.* She has exhibited her paintings
throughout Devon, works with visual artists, and in education and
her poetry has appeared in many anthologies.
www.roselle-angwin.co.uk

CHRIS TUTTON

Chris Tutton has published five collections of poetry (Avalanche),
and has written plays for stage and radio, two documentaries, a six part
situation comedy and numerous songs. He was resident poet on
Carlton Television, and his work has been featured on BBC Radio 4, 5
and 1, Channel 4, ITV and Channel 1. A winner of the Sunday Times
Interaction Community Theatre Prize, he is a regular performer and
workshop/master class leader at home and abroad. He is currently
employed on a major London-wide initiative to promote the Year of
Reading.
www.christutton.co.uk

JOHN SIDDIQUE

John Siddique is the author of 'The Prize' (Rialto) 'Poems from
a Northern Soul' (Crocus Books) editor of 'Transparency'
(Crocus Books) and co-editor of 'Four Fathers' (ROUTE) His
children's book 'Don't Wear it on Your Head.' (Peepal Tree)

was shortlisted for the CLPE Poetry Award. He gives readings, mentors and teaches creative writing in the UK and abroad. www.johnsiddique.co.uk

PASCALE PETIT

Pascale Petit's last two collections, *The Huntress* (Seren, 2005) and *The Zoo Father* (Seren, 2001) were both shortlisted for the TS Eliot Prize and were books of the year in the *Times Literary Supplement.* Her poetry has been published in journals in the UK, US and Australia and broadcast on Radio 3 and 4. She gives readings nationally and internationally, was co-founder of *Poetry London*, is the Royal Literary Fund Fellow at Middlesex University 2007-2008 and a Next Generation Poet. www.pascalepetit.co.uk

FIONA SAMPSON

Fiona Sampson has published fourteen books – poetry, philosophy of language and books on the writing process – of which the most recent are *Common Prayer* (Carcanet 2007) and *Writing for Self and Reflexivity* (Macmillan, 2005). Her awards include the Newdigate Prize; the 2006 Forward Prize shortlist and she has been widely translated, with eight books in translation, including *Travel Diary,* awarded the Zlaten Prsten (Macedonia). She contributes regularly to *The Guardian, The Irish Times* and other publications, and is the editor of *Poetry Review.*

ALISON BRACKENBURY

Alison Brackenbury was born in Lincolnshire in 1953 She now lives in Gloucestershire and works in the family metal finishing business. Her last collection was *Bricks and Ballads* (Carcanet 2004).

Her poems have appeared on Radio 3 and 4 and she has been published in many newspapers, magazines and anthologies, including *The Times Literary Supplement, The Independent, PN Review* and *Poetry London*. She won an Eric Gregory Award in 1982 and the Cholmondeley Award 1997.
www.alisonbrackenbury.co.uk

MARVIN CHEESEMAN

Marvin Cheeseman made his debut as a performance poet in 1998. He has won several poetry "slams" and performs at festivals and comedy venues around the country. His first poetry collection *Full Metal Jacket Potato* was published in 2000. Marvin's work has featured on BBC Radio 1, 2 and 4 and appeared on the BBC television poetry series *Whine Gums*. He has published a limerick collection entitled *Making Prawn Sandwiches for Roy Keane*. He runs workshops throughout the North of England.

PHILIP GROSS

Apart from poetry, Philip Gross writes fiction for young people, haiku, libretti, plays and radio short stories. His adult poetry up to and including the Whitbread-shortlisted *The Waiting Game* is collected in *Changes of Address* (Bloodaxe, 2001) followed by *Mappa Mundi* (2003) and *The Storm Garden* (2006). Since 2006 he has been Professor of Creative Writing at Glamorgan University. He has worked with composers, dancers and visual artists. *The Abstract Garden* (Old Stile Press, 2006) is a book-length project with engraver Peter Reddick.
www.philipgross.co.uk

MATTHEW SWEENEY

Matthew Sweeney has written nine books of poetry for adults, the most recent being *Black Moon* (Cape 2007) and *Sanctuary* (2004), three collections of poetry and two novels for children, and edited several anthologies. Translated into many languages, he gives readings throughout Britain and Europe, undertakes residencies, runs workshops for adults and children, reviews books and is a frequent contributor to BBC radio programmes. Awards include the Cholmondeley Award 1986 and the Prudence Farmer Prize 1984.
www.contemporarywriters.com

HELEN IVORY

Helen Ivory was born in Luton in 1969. She won an Eric Gregory Award in 1999, and was given an Arts Council Writer's Award in 2005. Her second Bloodaxe collection *The Dog in the Sky* was published in 2006. She is Academic Director and tutor of Creative Writing at Continuing Education at the UEA. She also teaches on the BA Creative Writng and MA Writing the Visual at Norwich Art School. She is a regular reviewer for Seam magazine and an Editor for the Poetry Archive.

JOOLZ DENBY

Joolz Denby is a poet, novelist, spoken-word artist, photographer and illustrative artist. She performs her work world wide and has appeared on BBC Radio 4 (including *Woman's Hour*) Radio 1 and on BBC 2. Awards include New Crime Writer of the Year Award for *Stone Baby* (Harper Collins) which was also short-listed for the John Cressey Award. She was short-listed for the Orange Prize 2005. She has written commissioned poetry for Yorkshire Forward, The

Royal Armouries and the Yorkshire Museum Service among others.
www.joolz-denby.co.uk

NII AYIKWEI PARKES

Nii Ayikwei Parkes is a Ghanian writer, socio-cultural commentator and advocate for African writing. A 2005 associate Writer-in-Residence on BBC Radio 3, Nii is the author of three poetry pamphlets, and is working on his first full collection of poems, *The Makings of You.* An excerpt of his recently completed novel is featured in the British Council's New Writing Anthology *NW15.* He contributes to journals and magazines and co-edited the short story anthologies, *Tell Tales.*
www.niiparkes.com

PHILIP COKER

Born in Liverpool in 1950 Philip Coker moved to Birmingham five years later where he still lives. He is currently Community Librarian at Hall Green Library where he chairs the Poetry Group, organises poetry events and was instrumental in forming Birmingham's Poetry Places. He has had poems published in *Ringside Verse* and on websites in both text and audio.

PAUL SUTHERLAND

Paul Sutherland, Canadian-British poet, came to the UK in 1973. He has five collections, the most recent being *Seven Earth Odes* (2004) and edited four others. He is the founder-editor of the literary magazine, *Dream Catcher* and attends festivals as a workshop leader. Poems have appeared in magazines including *Poetry New Zealand, Nassau Review* (USA) and *North Yorkshire 199.* He was writer in residence at the first Lincoln Book Festival.

KATRINA PORTEOUS

Katrina Porteous lives on the Northumberland coast. Her poetry collections include *The Lost Music* (Bloodaxe 1996), the long dialect poem *The Wind an' the Wetter* (Iron 1999), and radio-poems such as *Dunstanburgh* (Smokestack 2004) and *Longshore Drift* (Jardine Press 2005). She also writes social history, most recently *The Bonny Fisher Lad* (The People's History 2003). Katrina has been poet-in-residence in many locations, including the Shetland Isles, Newlyn Harbour and the Aldburgh Poetry Festival. www.katrinaporteous.co.uk

KOSTAS HRISOS

Kostas Hrisos was born in Greece, lives in Newcastle upon Tyne and teaches Information Systems and Creative Writing. His poems have been published in magazines and anthologies and he has read in Newcastle, London and Athens. A collection of his work *In Other Words* was published in 2000. He translated Basil Bunting's *Briggflatts* into Greek and is currently finishing his first novel. He is also responsible for interpoetry.com.

MARTIN FIGURA

Martin Figura was born in Liverpool in 1956 and works as a photographer. He also teaches on the BA Creative Wrting at Norwich Arts School. His second poetry collection *Ahem* was published by Eggbox in 2005. He is a member of the Joy of 6, a performance group, and has performed widely in the UK, and in New York and Toronto. He has been published in magazines in the UK and US and in 2006 won the Café Writers Poetry Competition.

ROZ GODDARD

Roz Goddard's first full collection of poetry, *How to Dismantle a Hotel Room,* was published in 2006 and her poetry has been broadcast on BBC Radio 3 and 4. During 2003-4 she was appointed Birmingham's poet laureate and first writer-in-residence for the Orange Birmingham Book Festival. She runs workshops and courses, most recently for the Arvon Foundation, with individual writers and gives readings across the country.
www.rozgoddard.com

DAVID HENDTLASS

David Hendtlass has written poetry, plays and a fantasy novel for children. His poetry has been included in magazines and anthologies, and he has staged and recorded a verse drama, *The Kings Road Mystery Play.* He is currently working on his first full collection of poems.

MAYA CHOWDHRY

Maya Chowdhry is a poet, playwright and inTer-aCt-ive artist creating lyrical texts for radio, the web, page and stage. Awards include the BBC Young Radio Playwights Festival with *Monsoon.* Her poetry has been published in several anthologies and magazines, on the web and CD; including *Healing Strategies for Women at War: Seven Black Women poets, The Redbeck Anthology of British South Asian Poetry, As Girls Could Boast;* new poetry by women and Ambit.
www.destinyNation.net

35636